THE SETTLE TO CARLISLE RAILWAY

Gordon Edgar

AMBERLEY

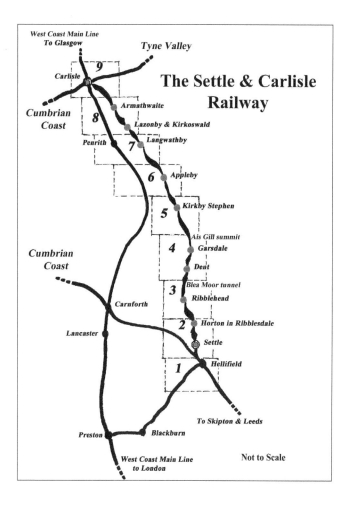

The Settle & Carlisle Railway

West Coast Main Line To Glasgow
Tyne Valley
Carlisle
9
Cumbrian Coast
8
Armathwaite
Lazonby & Kirkoswald
Penrith
7
Langwathby
6
Appleby
Kirkby Stephen
5
Ais Gill summit
4
Garsdale
Dent
3
Blea Moor tunnel
Ribblehead
Cumbrian Coast
Carnforth
2
Horton in Ribblesdale
Lancaster
Settle
1
Hellifield
To Skipton & Leeds
Preston
Blackburn
West Coast Main Line to London
Not to Scale

Front cover: The prospect of sun at the late Right Reverend Eric Treacy's favourite location could not be ignored on the last of this season's Winter Cumbrian Mountain Expresses, and what a fine sight the Scot made coming over the 'Roof of England' at an incredible speed. Highly appropriate for the line, Stanier Royal Scot Class 4-6-0 No. 46115 *Scots Guardsman* approaches the summit at Ais Gill heading the 'Winter Cumbrian Mountain Express', the 1Z87 14.40 from Carlisle to London Euston on Saturday 8 March 2014. [4]

Back cover: With the late-running 'Fellsman' charter from Carlisle to Lancaster heading across distant Batty Moss viaduct, Ribblehead, with Stanier 8F 2-8-0 No. 48151 in charge on 11 July 2013, the Middle Scar of Runscar Scar is pleasantly illuminated, with the backlit sunlight falling upon selective parts of the limestone landscape. [3]

First published 2014

Amberley Publishing
The Hill, Stroud
Gloucestershire, GL5 4EP

www.amberley-books.com

ISBN 978 1 4456 3961 1 (print)
ISBN 978 1 4456 3973 4 (ebook)

British Library Cataloguing in Publication Data.
A catalogue record for this book is available from the British Library.

Typeset in 9.5pt on 12pt Celeste.
Typesetting by Amberley Publishing.
Printed in the UK.

Introduction

The history of the Settle–Carlisle Railway (S&C) has been well documented in many previous publications over the years, and it is not my intention to emulate any of those fine historical works. Neither are the photographs in this book presented in a logical geographical fashion as one might expect, but rather grouped together in themes as much as possible, expressly with the intention of better conveying the immense drama and feeling of isolation as this tremendous railway wends its way along the backbone of England, the 73 miles from Settle Junction to Carlisle's Petteril Bridge Junction. That is not to say, however, that the fine stations of Carlisle Citadel and Hellifield should be ignored because they just fall outside of the officially recognised S&C route criterion.

The last fifteen years since railway privatisation are illustrated, providing a more recent pictorial overview rather than just a potted history of this iconic line. The S&C has indeed moved on from its charmed post-steam railway existence through the 1970s, its threat of closure hanging over it throughout most of the 1980s and its transition from nationalisation to privatisation in the 1990s. In fact the line has proved to be a real success story of the early twenty-first century, with increasing passenger revenues and freight traffic, so much so that expensive infrastructure upgrades have been deemed necessary to provide additional line capacity for heavier and more frequent trains. The downside of this of course has been the rationalisation of some station and siding areas, in turn involving the removal of traditional semaphore signalling, which had previously added to the line's traditional railway appearance. Additionally, the recent disappearance of a number of obsolete platelayer's huts, sidings and signal boxes has gone relatively unnoticed by the casual visitor. Despite these changes, the S&C still possesses much Victorian railway ambience and charm.

Special mention must be made here of the Friends of the Settle to Carlisle, who continue to actively campaign for a better service between Leeds and Carlisle. They regularly provide On Train Guides in order to enhance the travelling experience over the S&C, and also lead guided walks from stations along the line and at the historic Ribblehead site. The organisation also deserves credit for the magnificent presentation of the stations along the route, having been vigorously involved in fundraising and restoration projects for many years in order to present them in the condition that we can enjoy today. They take care of the station gardens, have provided the stations with heritage-style seating and Victorian lamps, and not least continue to protect the buildings from deterioration by regular repainting. The former national network signal boxes at Settle and Armathwaite were also taken over by the Friends when they became obsolete and are frequently made available to visitors at certain times. Their shops at Settle and Appleby stations also sell a wide variety of S&C-related items and local produce. The Settle–Carlisle Development Company also has an important part to play in promoting the line by handling retail management, leaflet/timetable production, expansion of ticket sales and the Dales Railcard scheme, and not least providing a refreshment trolley for passengers on certain services, enhancing the journey for the passengers.

The last fifteen years have been witness to previously unimaginable organic growth of rail freight, not only by traffic using the route as an alternative to the congested West Coast Main Line (WCML) but also for dispatching or receiving bulk commodities such as timber, stone and containerised gypsum. As contracts are renewed, freight operating companies continue to add to the rich tapestry of corporate liveries witnessed on the line, in stunning landscape unequalled elsewhere in the country. During the earlier days of privatisation, the efforts of Arriva Trains to reintroduce locomotive-hauled passenger services were regrettably short-lived and the return to diesel multiple units had been arguably short-sighted, certainly judging by the passenger footfall now experienced all the year round on many of the timetabled services. Charter and excursion trains visit the S&C in ever increasing numbers throughout the year and more often than not continue to be a sell-out success story, and long may that continue to be the case. Additionally, it is unimaginable that the S&C was scheduled for closure in the 1989, when it has proved to be in more recent times such a strategic diversionary route when the WCML is closed for engineering works.

It was really quite fitting that the final BR steam-hauled passenger train, the famous '15 Guinea' 1T57 special of 11 August 1968, ran over the S&C. It is also satisfying that, since the steam locomotive's return to the main line in 1971, the line has always been very well represented in the annual steam charter train calendar. Indeed, the 45th year anniversary of the '15 Guinea' special was marked with similar motive power, if not totally identical locomotives on the southbound working. The 50th anniversary undoubtedly promises to be equally exciting!

The so-called 'mountain' stretch of the line, chiefly that section between Ribblehead and Kirkby Stephen over the 'Roof of England', arguably offers the most challenges to man and machine, and also to the photographer, and as a result is well documented in this book. The immense drama of a steam locomotive with a trailing load of at times up to twelve coaches on the prevailing 1 in 100 gradients both north and southbound, pitted against the far-ranging elements, draws visitors to the line time after time. There is no other place like it in the country, despite the generally cloudy Pennine weather. However, on a good day the views are unequalled, perhaps more so during the winter months when the high fells can boast a dusting of snow and the visibility can be crystal clear.

The line continues to be ever popular with travellers and photographers alike. Indeed, the S&C has captured the imagination of many eminent photographers over the years, arguably the most famous of all being the Rt Revd Eric Tracy, former Bishop of Wakefield, who sadly passed away on Appleby station in May 1978 while waiting to photograph a steam charter working.

It is to be hoped that this book goes some way to convey the unequalled qualities of the S&C. From the green pastures and limestone outcrops of the southern area, the upland dales and far-reaching moorland of the central or 'mountain' section of the line around Ribblehead, Dent and Ais Gill, and the lush pastureland of the Eden Valley with its distinctive red Cumbrian sandstone outcrops, the Victorian railway feel about the whole line is quite unique on our national railway system today. In its status as an 'everyday working national monument' it is to be treasured and long may it survive and prosper.

All photographs featured in this book were taken by the author. For the assistance of those readers who are unfamiliar with the line's geography, the S&C route has been divided into nine random sectors on a map, and at the end of each photograph caption there follows a corresponding number referring to the section of line within which the photograph was taken.

Below: Gresley K4 Mogul No. 61994 *The Great Marquess* fills the rock cutting at Waitby with exhaust, clinging in the falling rain and sheltered from the strong easterly wind. This was the return 'Fellsman' charter to Lancaster from Carlisle on Wednesday 15 August 2012. [5]

GB Railfreight's 66712 is in charge of the 6M20 Drax to Newbiggin, loaded with containerised gypsum, crossing Smardale viaduct near Crosby Garrett on 10 August 2005. The gypsum is a by-product of the desulphurisation process at the power station and is processed to produce raw plaster at British Gypsum's Kirkby Thore works. [5]

With heavy rain falling on the northern Pennines in the distance, Network Rail's HST 'New Management Train' (NMT) heads north near to Stockber on Saturday 28 July 2012. [5]

Virgin's celebrity two-tone green-liveried Class 47 No. 47851 *Traction Magazine* heads the 1M22 11.40 Carlisle–Preston through the misty Eden Valley at Armathwaite on 17 January 2004. [8]

The rain showed no sign of abating at Ais Gill summit on Thursday 15 August 2013 as Direct Rail Services (DRS) 37405 (with 37419 on the rear) worked the 1Q13 Carnforth Down Sidings–Kingmoor TMD test train, passing the location so familiar to many, but looking in the direction of the classic photographic viewpoint. Ais Gill is a watershed, close to the source of the rivers Ure and Eden, the former running through North Yorkshire and into the River Ouse, and the latter flowing on to the Border City, Carlisle, and into the Solway Firth. [4]

Above: BR Class 8P Pacific No. 71000 *Duke of Gloucester* in charge of the northbound Cumbrian Mountain Express to Carlisle at Selside on 19 May 2011, overlooked by the leonine summit of Pen-y-ghent, 2,273 feet above sea level. [3]

Below: Doyen of the BR Britannia Class 7P6F Pacifics, No. 70000 *Britannia*, charges off the Arten Gill viaduct high above Dentdale on the Settle–Carlisle line, heading the 1Z70 London King's Cross–Carlisle charter on 3 March 2012, with steam haulage from York to Carlisle. The viaduct, arguably the Settle–Carlisle's most dramatic in terms of its setting betwixt Dent Fell and Dentdale, was built from locally hewn dark grey limestone rock containing millions of white fossils. [3]

Threatening skies, so commonplace in the area, overshadow Stanier Jubilee Class 4-6-0 No. 5690 *Leander* as it storms away from Batty Moss viaduct towards Blea Moor tunnel on 12 August 2009. [3]

The splendour of the lower Eden Valley can be fully appreciated in this view of Stanier Black 5 No. 44871 heading a York–Carlisle 'Waverley' charter at Long Strumble on 5 September 2010. [9]

The driver of Royal Scot Class 4-6-0 No. 46115 *Scots Guardsman*, heading the 'Thames-Clyde Express', waves to the signalman at Garsdale signal box as the train thunders through the deserted platform. This was the 1Z79 07.58 Scarborough–Carlisle private charter on Saturday 23 June 2012. Garsdale, known as Hawes Junction station until 1932, was one of only two true junction stations on the Settle–Carlisle line (the other being Penrith Junction at Appleby) and also boasted an island platform serving the Hawes and Northallerton line through Wensleydale. Originally it was a key point where pilot locomotives were removed from double-headed trains and then returned to Hellifield or Carlisle. The signal box in this scene was brought into use in 1910 and boasted a forty-lever frame. It will eventually be taken out of service under the proposed Network Rail resignalling scheme for the line and, as a listed structure, is anticipated to become a museum. [4]

Gresley A4 Pacific No. 60009 *Union of South Africa* rounds the curve at Duncowfold, milepost 302 from St Pancras, and nearly journey's end on the northbound 'Cumbrian Mountain Express' to Carlisle on Saturday 31 August 2013. [9]

Stanier Jubilee 4-6-0 5690 *Leander* storms through Kirkby Stephen station heading a return 'Fellsman' charter from Carlisle to Lancaster on 8 September 2000. The Midland Railway station, originally named Kirkby Stephen West, is at an elevation of 890 feet and built to the same specification as Settle and Appleby, but that is where the similarity ends, for it is a mile and a half from the town and elevated 150 feet higher! It was closed in 1970 but reopening came about in 1986. [5]

Although the 'Cathedrals Explorer' was 165 minutes down on its booked time at this stage, the low evening light at Cumwhinton was indeed a bonus. Storm clouds are starting to brew inland as 4464 *Bittern* purrs along, attempting to regain some of its lost time on the 1Z44 from Carlisle to Hellifield, originating as the 1Z43 from Edinburgh to Carlisle on 24 May 2012. The station closed in 1956 and is now a private dwelling with a well-tended garden. [9]

Gresley K4 2-6-0 No. 61994 *The Great Marquess* emits a pleasing amount of exhaust for such a warm day at Ling Gill as she heads down the 1 in 330 gradient from Rise Hill tunnel in charge of the 'Fellsman' charter from Lancaster to Carlisle on Wednesday 24 July 2013. [4]

Stanier Black 5, 4-6-0 No. 45231 *The Sherwood Forester*, heads towards Moorcock Tunnel at Garsdale Head with the 1Z52 07.08 Lancaster–Carlisle 'Fellsman' charter on Wednesday 3 July 2013. The arch-relieved wing walls of the skew arch bridge, constructed in 1872, are noteworthy. [4]

Above: Gresley A4 Pacific No. 60009 *Union of South Africa* runs out of the short London Road tunnel and through the suburbs of Carlisle, near its outward destination, heading the 1Z21 Crewe to Carlisle 'Cumbrian Mountain Express' on Saturday 14 September 2013. [9]

Left: As soon as 61264 and 45407 are clear of London Road Tunnel, a whistle from the B1 signals for the regulators to be opened. On wet rails and in dismal conditions, the Class 5 mixed-traffic duo make an impressive sight storming away from the Border City towards Petteril Bridge Junction and the Settle–Carlisle route. The first Winter Cumbrian Mountain Express of the 2014 season. [9]

DRS 66434 (still bearing the Jarvis Fastline decals) is towing failed Colas Rail 66845 and is drawing away from the isolated, exposed location of Ribblehead with a loaded timber train for Chirk on 21 May 2011. [3]

DB Schenker (DBS) 66201 heads the 4M00 07.05 Mossend–Clitheroe 'Castle Cement' empties through Horton-in-Ribblesdale on 19 May 2011. [2]

Colas Rail 66850 heads the 6J37 Carlisle Yard–Chirk timber at Bullgill, just south of Kirkby Stephen, on 24 February 2012. [5]

DBS 66099 heads the 6K05 12.18 Carlisle Yard–Crewe departmental service over Arten Gill viaduct on 11 August 2011. [3]

Royal Scot Class 4-6-0 No. 46115 *Scots Guardsman* on the 1 in 132 climb at Lockhills, approaching Armathwaite station, heading the return 'Waverley' charter from Carlisle to York on Sunday 4 August 2013. [8]

Stanier Black 5, 45407 *The Lancashire Fusilier*, storms towards Armathwaite tunnel at milepost 297 heading a Carlisle–York return 'Waverley' charter on 8 August 2010. [8]

LMS-liveried Coronation 4-6-2 No. 6233 *Duchess of Sutherland* emerges from Crosby Garrett tunnel heading a southbound 'Cumbrian Mountain Express' on 24 July 2010. This short tunnel, only 181 yards long, was built between 1873 and 1875. [5]

The rosebay willowherb was at its most vibrant, adding colour to an otherwise mostly dismal day, perhaps reflecting the sombre mood forty-five years ago when the two Black 5s heading south over the Settle–Carlisle line, as far as everyone thought at the time, marked the end of mainline steam in the UK. What a wonderful sight this was: 45231 and 44932 opening up on the 1 in 330 climb after the temporary speed restriction at Garsdale, returning the 1T57 '15 Guinea Special' from Carlisle to Liverpool Lime Street on Sunday 11 August 2013. [4]

Royal Scot Class 4-6-0 No. 46115 *Scots Guardsman* arrives at Carlisle Citadel station heading the 'Fellsman' charter from York on 27 July 2011. The children running down the platform as the Scot arrives took the author right back to the previous time that he actually saw the locomotive at this station, in August 1965, some forty-six years previously, virtually to the day! [9]

As a Carlisle area resident, one charter train diagram that the author just could not ignore documenting in the Border City was a 08.21 departure for Blackpool from 'The Citadel'. It was unthinkable, with the cessation of steam on BR forty-five years previously, that such a spectacle would be possible in 2013. The fine surviving Crown Street cast-iron bridge structure is seen in the foreground as Stanier Black 5, 44932 of 10A Carnforth shed, heads the 1Z43 05.48 Kilmarnock–Blackpool 'Fylde Coast Express' on Wednesday 22 May 2013, making an impressive departure with Carlisle-resident and Driver Gordon Hodgson on the regulator. [9]

Right: The interconnecting passages between platforms 1 and 3 at Carlisle Citadel station can provide interesting cameos, but how the eventual composition turns out is very much in the lap of the gods and there's no action replay – not for at least a week anyway! Stanier Coronation 4-6-2 No. 46233 *Duchess of Sutherland* rolls into the station heading the 1Z31 'Royal Scot' charter train from Milton Keynes on Saturday 9 June 2012, given hardly a second glance by three teenage girls heading for their Cumbrian Coast service train, but conversely, two more senior 'girls' sitting on the platform seat are caught waving frantically to the fireman, just as they would have done fifty years ago. [9]

Below: Stanier Black 5, 4-6-0 No. 45305, propels the empty stock for the 'Mersey Moorlander' charter out of the shunt neck beneath St Nicholas Bridge, Carlisle, on 30 July 2012. The long road bridge crosses the Tyne Valley and Settle–Carlisle routes at this point, and the freight-avoiding lines at Bog Junction are to the bottom left of the photograph while the West Coast Main Line is beyond at a higher level. [9]

With Mount Zion chapel prominent, on a dismal and wet day that is so typical of the area, Stanier Black 5, 4-6-0 No. 45231 *The Sherwood Forester*, races across Dandry Mire viaduct heading the Lancaster–Carlisle 'Fellsman' charter on Wednesday 3 July 2013. The Mount Zion chapel (also known as the Hawes Junction chapel), Garsdale Head, was opened in 1876, the same year that passenger traffic began on the Settle–Carlisle line, and served a local community of railway employees and farmers. The chapel is strategically placed at a confluence of the dales, and services are still occasionally held. [4]

Conveying the mood of the occasion, Stanier Jubilee 4-6-0 45699 *Galatea* battles against the strong wind and horizontal sleet as it approaches Kirkby Stephen station with the southbound 'Winter Cumbrian Express' on Saturday 1 February 2014. [5]

Stanier Black 5, 4-6-0 No. 44932, forges through the heavy rain at Shotlock Hill in charge of the 1Z60 08.51 York–Carlisle 'Waverley' charter on Saturday 6 August 2011. [4]

Stanier Jubilee Class 4-6-0 No. 45699 *Galatea*, with the late-running 1Z87 14.44 Carlisle–London Euston 'Winter Cumbrian Mountain Express', bursts out of Armathwaite tunnel and storms up the 1 in 220 gradient to Baron Wood summit on a wet Saturday 8 February 2014. [8]

Gresley A4 Pacific No. 60009 *Union of South Africa* runs through Carlisle's Citadel station platform 3, arriving with a 'Cumbrian Mountain Express', the 1Z86 originating from London Euston, on 9 March 2013. The station was opened in 1847 and later extended, and is close to the highest station in England. Seven railway companies, including the Midland Railway from the Settle–Carlisle route, operated from it. [9]

A number of becks run off the lower eastern slopes of Whernside and Blea Moor to form Winterscales Beck and the Greta headwaters. These include Force Gill, which runs over the aqueduct near to the mouth of Blea Moor tunnel. On the totally overcast morning of Wednesday 28 August 2013 Gresley K4 2-6-0 No. 61994 *The Great Marquess* fights the grade to Blea Moor tunnel, crossing Little Dale Beck, in charge of the final 'Fellsman' Lancaster–Carlisle charter of the season. [3]

Stanier Black 5, 4-6-0 No. 45231 *The Sherwood Forester,* and Brush Type 4 No. D1762 (Class 47 47580) head towards Blea Moor up outer home signal with the 'Fellsman' charter in appalling conditions on Wednesday 31 July 2013, as the tail of the 4S00 Clitheroe–Mossend cement train just clears the view. [3]

Against the gloom of Risehill, a brief shaft of sunlight places the spotlight on Stanier Black 5 Nos 45231 and 44932 as they climb away from Garsdale onto the level section, site of the erstwhile Garsdale water troughs, heading the return 1T57 '15 Guinea Special' from Carlisle to Liverpool Lime Street on Sunday 11 August 2013. [4]

With the distinctive mass of Ingleborough looming beyond, DBS 66021 has a storm chasing its tail as it heads the 4S93 15.04 Milford–Hunterston coal empties near Blea Moor. [3]

English Welsh & Scottish Railway (EWS) 'Dutch'-liveried 37350 heading a Gascoigne Wood–Carlisle London Road Cawood's containerised coal train at Ais Gill summit on 29 May 1999. The volume of cars parked at the summit hints at a southbound steam-hauled charter being imminent! [4]

DBS 66102 labours away from Blea Moor signal box towards the 2,629-yard tunnel heading the 6S00 Clitheroe–Mossend cement on 21 August 2013. [3]

Just as the sun has risen high enough above Widdale Fell to illuminate upper Dentdale, EWS 60079 *Foinaven* (with Mainline sector decals) heads northbound MGR empties across the eleven-arch Arten Gill viaduct early on 4 September 1999. [4]

The northbound 'Fellsman' charter with Stanier Jubilee 4-6-0 45699 *Galatea* at the head passing the delightful High Scale farmhouse on Wednesday 18 July 2013, with Garsdale and Rise Hill beyond. [4]

Stanier Black 5 No. 45157 *The Lancashire Fusilier* (aka 45407) romps across Batty Moss viaduct heading the 09.10 Liverpool Lime Street–Carlisle 'Cumbrian Fellsman' on 23 October 2000. [3]

As a heavy downpour sheets northwards towards Langwathby, Stanier 8F 2-8-0 No. 48151 forges through the rain at the skew bridge on the climb to Wastebank tunnel, crossing the fertile flatlands where the rivers Eamont (from Ullswater) and Eden meet. This was the return 1Z53 15.34 Carlisle–Lancaster 'Fellsman' charter on 4 July 2012. [7]

The last of the afternoon sunlight, proving to be an extremely rare commodity in early 2014, showcases Royal Scot Class 4-6-0 No. 46115 *Scots Guardsman* as it tackles the grade towards the 'Roof of England', high above Crosby Garrett village, with the 1Z87 Carlisle–Farington Junction and London Euston on Saturday 15 February 2014. [5]

EWS 37408 *Loch Rannoch* and 37411, on hire to Arriva Trains, 'top and tail' a Carlisle to Leeds stopping service, powering across Eden Lacy viaduct (otherwise known as Long Meg viaduct) near Great Salkeld on a crisp 29 December 2003. The Settle–Carlisle line crosses the River Eden in just two places: here and at Ormside viaduct south of Appleby. [7]

Virgin Trains Thunderbird Class 57/3 No. 57305 *John Tracy* crosses Armathwaite viaduct heading a diverted Euston–Glasgow service on 17 January 2004. [8]

Above: EWS 37408 *Loch Rannoch* heads an Arriva Trains Carlisle–Leeds afternoon service at Armathwaite on 29 January 2004. [8]

Below: On 17 January 2004, a diverted West Coast Anglo-Scottish Virgin Voyager service heads south through the Eden Valley at Armathwaite as the mist rises from the River Eden. [8]

Class A2 Pacific No. 60532 *Blue Peter* speeds past Watershed Mill, north of Settle, heading the 09.20 Crewe–Carlisle 'Cumbrian Mountain Express' on 1 May 2000. [2]

The final 'Waverley' charter of the 2012 season, behind Stanier Black 5 No. 45305, crossing the majestic 80-foot-high Dry Beck viaduct with the 1Z73 15.45 Carlisle–York on 9 September 2012. [8]

While not strictly on the official S&C route, Hellifield, located between Settle Junction and Carlisle and a mere 4 miles south of the Junction, with its superbly restored Midland Railway island platform station and a glimpse of Pendle Hill, surely deserves a place in this book. Passing the narrow signal box at the south end, Stanier Black 5, 4-6-0 No. 45157 *The Lancashire Fusilier* (aka 45407), takes the Blackburn line out of Hellifield with the return S&C 125th Anniversary Special to Manchester Victoria from Carlisle on 1 May 2001. [1]

Royal Scot Class 4-6-0 No. 46115 *Scots Guardsman* emerges from Armathwaite Tunnel heading the first York–Carlisle 'Waverley' charter of the summer 2013 season on Sunday 28 July 2013. Also known as Cat Clint Tunnel, it is 325 yards in length, with one 50-foot-deep ventilation shaft, built between 1870 and 1871. [8]

There was overnight freezing rain in Cumbria and North Yorkshire on 9 February 2012, causing widespread road accidents. With temperatures hovering around zero, the raindrops froze into ice as they hit the ground, producing the most hazardous surface conditions imaginable, although this eventually turned to snow. Much of the ice still remained two days later, making negotiating a way through the grikes and clints of these limestone pavements at Ribblehead even more lethal than normal. Following a signal check to allow an Up Northern Rail service to pass at Ribblehead station, Britannia Class 4-6-2 No. 70013 *Oliver Cromwell* gets briskly into its stride heading the 1Z87 winter 'Cumbrian Mountain Express', the 11.06 from Preston to Carlisle, on 11 February 2012. [3]

Runscar Scar is the main feature of this landscape image, with Stanier 8F 2-8-0 48151 descending over Batty Moss viaduct, Ribblehead, from Blea Moor tunnel with the 1Z53 15.34 Carlisle–Lancaster 'Fellsman' charter on 10 July 2013. [3]

Just after midday on 19 December 2000, and in driving rain and a gale-force wind, Stanier 8F 2-8-0 No. 48151 draws a loaded ballast train slowly but positively across Batty Moss viaduct, a special working from Ribblehead sidings to Carlisle Yard. Nothing like this had been witnessed since the late 1960s and will most likely never ever be seen again. This was truly a remarkable occasion, despite the weather conditions and the unforgiving wind carrying the locomotive's exhaust in advance of its progress. Indeed, this was classic Settle–Carlisle weather and arguably nothing else would have sufficed. [3]

BR 8P Pacific No. 71000 *Duke of Gloucester*, heading the 1Z63 10.50 York–Carlisle 'Cumbrian Mountain Express', crossing the impressive twenty-four-arch Batty Moss viaduct at Ribblehead, viewed from the rain-washed limestone escarpment on the eastern side on 14 October 2006. Ribblehead viaduct in North Yorkshire is arguably the most impressive structure on the Settle–Carlisle Line, and certainly world-famous. Hundreds of railway builders ('navvies') lost their lives building the line, in a combination of accidents, fights, and smallpox outbreaks, and the building of the Batty Moss viaduct caused such loss of life that the railway paid for an expansion of the local graveyard. Memorials along the line, especially those at St Mary's church, Outhgill, and St Leonard's church, Chapel-le-Dale, commemorate the lives of some of the men who died building the line. [3]

Deltic Class 55 D9009 *Alycidon* heads a northbound charter to Appleby across Smardale viaduct on 13 June 1999. The twelve-arch Smardale viaduct, at 131 feet, is the highest on the line and has foundations sunk 45 feet below ground. The completion of the viaduct was celebrated by a carved stone which was tapped into place on 8 June 1875 by Agnes Crossley, wife of the line's engineer, John Crossley. Under the arches is the trackbed of the former NER line from Kirkby Stephen to Tebay, now a public footpath. [5]

Deltic Class 55 D9000 *Royal Scots Grey*, on hire to Virgin Trains, heading the 07.38 Glasgow–Bournemouth across Arten Gill viaduct on 27 February 1999, diverted from the West Coast Main Line (WCML) service via the Settle–Carlisle line. [3]

A north-easterly wind blows across Dandry Mire as Stanier 8F 2-8-0 No. 48151 leaves an exhaust trail behind its coaches trundling over the viaduct at Garsdale Head, heading a 'Fellsman' charter from Lancaster to Carlisle on Wednesday 10 July 2013. Dandry Mire viaduct, comprising twelve arches, was completed following vain attempts to build an embankment, the Mire proving too difficult to work with. [4]

EWS Class 60 No. 60055 *Thomas Barnardo* heads an up MGR approaching Garsdale on 5 June 1999, at the point where the branch to Hawes used to join the Settle–Carlisle line. [4]

The small beck beneath the lofty seven-arch viaduct at Dry Beck was far from dry at the time this image was taken, following several weeks of seemingly incessant rainfall. The viaduct, 80 feet high and 139 yards long, is on a northbound rising gradient of 1 in 132. The majestic structure was built between 1871 and 1874. The Lancaster–Carlisle 'Fellsman' charter, with Stanier 8F 2-8-0 No. 48151 in charge, crosses the viaduct on Wednesday 11 July 2012. [8]

Judging by the way some of the remaining telegraph poles are now leaning on this section of the Settle–Carlisle Line it will probably not be too long before they are removed on safety grounds, in much the same way that the former platelayer's lineside huts are gradually being eradicated. Stanier Royal Scot Class 4-6-0 No. 46115 *Scots Guardsman* is heading the York–Carlisle 'Waverley' charter at Low Cotehill on Sunday 4 August 2013. [9]

Stanier Princess Class 4-6-2 No. 6201 *Princess Elizabeth* passes Greengate, south of Kirkby Stephen, well into the relentless and consistent 1 in 100 climb to Ais Gill summit with the 1Z20 06.09 Crewe–Carlisle 'Cumbrian Mountain Express' on 31 July 2010. [5]

With a pleasing, work-worn appearance, Stanier 8F 2-8-0 No. 48151 approaches Birkett Tunnel heading a Carlisle–Preston return 'Fellsman' charter on 18 August 2010. Constructed through the Great Pennine Fault between 1871 and 1874, the tunnel is 424 yards long. [5]

Class 31 Nos 31601 and 31454 head the late-running 1Z56 Lincoln–Carlisle 'Rail Blue Charter' at Staingill near Langwathby on 2 March 2011. [7]

DBS 67025 *Western Star* forges through the rain at the Howe & Co. sidings on the last leg of its outward journey to Carlisle with a 'Rail Blue' charter train from London Euston on 30 October 2010. [9]

Above: Western Class 52 diesel-hydraulic No. D1015 *Western Champion* passes Birkett Green near Kirkby Stephen on its ground-breaking journey over the Settle–Carlisle Line on 31 July 2010. It was to be three more years before it was to make a return to Cumbria. [5]

Below: DB Schenker-liveried 67018 *Keith Heller* passes London Road Junction on the approach to Carlisle heading the 1Z69 'Rail Blue' charter from Harlow on 27 April 2011. [9]

Stanier Jubilee Class 4-6-0 No. 45699 *Galatea* made a welcome return to Carlisle on 23 October 2013. This was the very first Jubilee that the author saw, at Eastleigh motive power depot on the Southern Region of all places, in 1964, just prior to its despatch to Woodham's scrapyard at Barry. Evoking memories of Summer Saturday extras at Carlisle, *Galatea* makes a spirited start from the Border City, opening up just clear of London Road tunnel heading the return 'Cumbrian Mountain Express' to London Euston via the Settle–Carlisle Line. [9]

Leaving a very dismal and wet Carlisle behind, Bulleid un-rebuilt Battle of Britain Pacific No. 34067 *Tangmere* is doing what it is well renowned for, leaving a clag trail in its wake, climbing up the 1 in 132 grade at Cumwhinton while heading the return 1Z87 'Cumbrian Mountain Express' charter to London Euston on 12 April 2012. [9]

It is painfully evident in this bird's-eye view of Culgaith Crossing (one of just two on the Settle–Carlisle line) how 'jungle-like' lineside vegetation is gradually consuming our scenic railways. A 1983 photograph taken by the late-Roger Siviter in his book entitled *The Settle to Carlisle – a Tribute* makes for an interesting comparison and reveals that not one tree or large shrub is evident along this complete stretch of line. At least the signal box, two semaphores (one out of view) and the station clock still survive as a reminder of happier times, although the station closed in 1970. Gresley A4 Pacific 60009 *Union of South Africa* approaches the crossing heading the 1Z21 Crewe–Carlisle 'Cumbrian Mountain Express' on Saturday 4 August 2012. [7]

Peppercorn A1 Pacific No. 60163 *Tornado* rounds the curve at Low Cotehill on the 1 in 132 climb to Armathwaite heading the 1Z62 15.45 'Cathedrals Express' from Carlisle to Crewe and London Euston on 31 May 2012. [9]

The fireman of Gresley K4 No. 61994 *The Great Marquess* is really shovelling on the coal for the climb ahead over 'The Roof of England' as the 1Z52 08.07 Lancaster–Carlisle 'Fellsman' charter makes its way towards Blea Moor Tunnel on the 1 in 100 climb away from Batty Moss viaduct on 8 August 2012. [3]

A work-weary Stanier Black 5 No. 44996 (aka 45407) approaches the former station of Cumwhinton heading a 1Z76 return 'Cumbrian Mountain Express' charter to Derby from Carlisle on 23 October 2004. [9]

Stanier Black 5 No. 45157 *The Lancashire Fusilier* (aka 45407) rounds the curve into Hellifield station heading the return 'S&C 125th Anniversary' charter to Manchester Victoria from Carlisle on 1 May 2001. [1]

The mass of Whernside enshrouded in cloud looms over Batty Moss viaduct and the Railway Inn at Ribblehead, a renowned and favourite watering hole for walkers, cavers, climbers and photographers alike, as DBS 66103 crosses on time heading the 4M00 Mossend–Clitheroe cement empties on Wednesday 5 March 2014. A Class 66 crossing the viaduct is highly appropriate for bridge 66, as it was simply known to the Settle–Carlisle engineers. Built of locally quarried limestone, it is the most imposing structure on the whole line. It is 104 feet high and 440 yards long and comprises twenty-four arches with piers 6 feet thick, except for every sixth pier, which is 18 feet thick and incorporated as a safety measure. [3]

With heavy rain clouds looming over Wild Boar Fell (2,324 feet), Freightliner Heavyhaul's 66526 *Driver Steve Dunn (George)* breasts Ais Gill Summit, at 1,169 feet above sea level, heading the 6Z68 Killoch–Drax loaded with coal on 4 July 2012. The signal box that at one time was sited on the Down side at the summit is now preserved by the Midland Railway Trust at Butterley in Derbyshire. [4]

Colas Rail's 56302 throbs up the 1 in 100 gradient past milepost 304 at Cumwhinton heading the 6J37 Carlisle Yard–Chirk (Kronospan) loaded with timber on Tuesday 28 May 2013. The logs are transported predominantly by road from the Kielder Forest to Kingmoor Yard for eventual processing into chipboard furniture products. [9]

DBS 66161 passes Howe & Co. sidings heading the 6K05 12.18 Carlisle Yard–Crewe Basford Hall Engineer's service on 15 September 2010. The sidings formerly served the British Gypsum factory at Cocklakes, with a short branch line worked by Andrew Barclay steam and diesel locomotives. [9]

With safety valves feathering and running in perfect form, Stanier Princess Class 4-6-2 No. 6201 *Princess Elizabeth* glides across Eden Lacy viaduct on the level, heading the return 1Z91 14.41 Carlisle–Tyseley Warwick Road 'Cumbrian Mountaineer' on Saturday 17 November 2012. [7]

After a perfect autumnal day in Cumbria on 27 October 2012, just an hour or so before the departure of the return 'Hadrian' charter to York, the clouds rolled in from the Irish Sea. A 16.54 departure from Carlisle at this time of year was always going to be a hit-and-miss affair, however the setting sun did produce some colour in the clouds and sufficient light to pick out the side of Gresley A4 4-6-2 60009 *Union of South Africa* as it rounded the curve approaching Armathwaite Tunnel. [8]

Seen from beneath the former Hawes branch line, Stanier Black 5, 4-6-0 No. 45231 *The Sherwood Forester*, heads the 1Z52 07.08 Lancaster–Carlisle 'Fellsman' charter across Dandry Mire viaduct on Wednesday 21 August 2013. [4]

Twenty minutes after sunset and following a sharp hailstorm, DRS 47832 *Solway Princess*, with Driver Mike Wylie at the helm, powers through Garsdale heading the 1Z55 11.42 Darlington–Carlisle–Newcastle 'Northern Belle' on Monday 3 December 2012. |4|

The overbridge and trackbed of the former Hawes branch from Hawes Junction at Garsdale Head marks the foreground for this image of DBS 66103 crossing Dandry Mire viaduct heading the 6M00 Mossend–Clitheroe with empty cement tanks on Wednesday 17 July 2013. [4]

DBS 66111 (with classmate 66115 dead in train) is in charge of the lightly loaded 6K05 12.18 Carlisle Yard–Crewe departmental service passing Selside on 19 May 2011. [3]

With a dusting of snow on Mallerstang Edge, DBS 66104, with grubby sister 66067 in tow, approaches the summit at Ais Gill heading the 6K05 12.18 Carlisle Yard–Crewe Basford Hall yard departmental on 10 November 2010. [4]

The sun is just setting, lighting up the northern sky with its warm colours, somewhat at odds with the temperature on the ground but curiously matching the colours of the Colas-liveried Class 66 No. 66849 *Wylam Dilly*, approaching the summit at Ais Gill, 1,169 feet above sea level. The sky is as black as night beyond and the driver of the Carlisle–Chirk timber train faces a hailstorm ahead, with it battering onto his cab window. The temperature here on 3 December 2012 was hovering just slightly above freezing. This is the unrivalled atmosphere of the 'Midland Route' over the roof of England during the winter months. [4]

At 72 miles and 46 chains from Settle Junction, Petteril Bridge Junction marks the most northerly point of the Settle–Carlisle Line. Near journey's end, Stanier Black 5, 4-6-0 No. 45305, rounds the curve and crosses the River Petteril heading the 1Z80 07.19 Liverpool Lime Street–Carlisle 'Mersey Moorlander' on Monday 30 July 2012. [9]

In far from ideal conditions for being out and about, with falling sleet, Gresley A4 Pacific No. 60009 *Union of South Africa* storms the climb to Ais Gill summit at Sycamore Tree Farm, high above Outhgill and the only settlement in the dale, heading the 1Z88 14.40 Carlisle–London Euston return 'Cumbrian Mountain Express' on Saturday 23 February 2013. [5]

Stanier Royal Scot Class 4-6-0 No. 46115 *Scots Guardsman* is well into its stride heading the 1Z86 15.02 Carlisle–Leicester Up 'Cumbrian Mountain Express', seen near Duncowfold on Saturday 25 June 2011. [9]

With Pen-y-ghent (2,273 feet) seemingly producing its own clag trail in competition, the lively Royal Scot Class 4-6-0 No. 46115 *Scots Guardsman* emits its distinctive three-cylinder symphony as it storms up the grade at High Birkwith, between Selside and Ribblehead, on 20 July 2011, heading the 1Z48 08.08 Lancaster–Carlisle 'Fellsman' charter. The wreath on the front of the locomotive was carried in tribute to John Shuttleworth, an eminent steam railway photographer, who sadly died after a long illness on 6 June 2011 at the age of seventy-one. [3]

Stanier Royal Scot Class 4-6-0 No. 46115 *Scots Guards*man at Low Moor, near Selside, heading the 1Z41 05.35 Stevenage–Carlisle excursion on 21 May 2011. [3]

On a glorious late summer's day, Stanier Jubilee 4-6-0 No. 5690 *Leander* looks splendid passing the site of the former Garsdale water troughs, high above the dale, heading the 1Z22 08.08 Lancaster–Carlisle 'Fellsman' charter on 1 September 2010. [4]

Britannia Class Pacific No. 70013 *Oliver Cromwell* approaches Birkett Tunnel on the climb from Kirkby Stephen to Ais Gill summit heading the 1Z87 14.37 Carlisle–London Euston 'Winter Cumbrian Mountain Express' charter on 31 March 2012. [5]

DBS 66113 heads the 6K05 12.18 Carlisle Yard–Crewe departmental at Selside Shaw on 18 August 2010. [3]

DRS 66421 (on spot-hire to Colas Rail) heads the 6J37 Carlisle Yard–Chirk loaded with timber at Selside Shaw on 19 May 2011. [3]

There was the unusual sight of Class 66/4 No. 66434, a former Jarvis Fastline locomotive, on the Settle–Carlisle Line on 21 May 2011. The DRS locomotive, acquired after the demise of Jarvis Fastline, came to the rescue of Colas Rail's 66845, which is being towed on the rear of the 6Z37 Ribblehead–Chirk loaded with timber, seen passing Selside Shaw. [3]

Colas Rail's Class 47 No. 47739 *Robin of Templecombe* powers the inaugural timber train, the 6Z41 from Ribblehead to Chirk, on 13 August 2010. The Class 47 ran round the train at Blea Moor to gain access to the Up line in order to proceed south, and then crossed the viaduct again forty minutes later, by which time darkness was falling. [3]

Stanier Duchess Pacific No. 46233 *Duchess of Sutherland* crosses Smardale viaduct in style, heading the 1Z27 07.05 Liverpool Lime Street–Carlisle 'Cumbrian Mountain Express' on Saturday 28 July 2012. Beneath the viaduct runs Scandal Beck, meandering from Ravenstonedale towards the Eden. [4]

Stanier Black 5, 4-6-0 No. 45407 *The Lancashire Fusilier*, is on the 1 in 100 climb near Selside, heading the 1Z60 09.32 York–Carlisle 'Waverley' on 24 July 2011. [3]

During a brief but welcome bright break in the clouds, Stanier Jubilee Class 4-6-0 No. 45699 *Galatea* crosses Batty Moss viaduct, glimpsed from Gunnerfleet Farm, with the 1Z40 06.30 Broxbourne–Carlisle 'Cathedrals Express' charter on Wednesday 5 March 2014. [3]

Gresley A4 Pacific No. 60009 *Union of South Africa* climbs the final mile up to Ais Gill summit at Mallerstang, heading the southbound 1Z88 14.40 Carlisle–London Euston 'Winter Cumbrian Mountain Express' on 16 February 2013. [4]

The 1Z20 Stratford-upon-Avon–Carlisle 'Black Cat' charter had DRS Class 20/3s Nos 20308 and 20309 up front and is seen at Duncowfold, in the lush Eden Valley, heading a varied rake of coaching stock. [9]

DRS 37218 and 37609 drift down the 1 in 100 grade at Wharton Dykes heading the 1Z37 12.42 Bristol Temple Meads–Carlisle 'Winter Settler' Pathfinder tour on Saturday 9 February 2013. [5]

The grazing meadows were finally showing some signs of recovery following an extended and unusual period of drought for so early in the year. West Coast Railway Co. No. 57316, still in the pleasing Arriva Trains Wales blue livery, heads the 1Z68 return 'Statesman' charter to Hull from Carlisle near Duncowfold on Saturday 27 April 2013. [9]

With snow-covered Cross Fell (the highest of the Pennine hills at 2,930 feet) and Great Dun Fell with its Civil Aviation Authority radar station dominating the backdrop, EWS 47757 *Capability Brown*, on hire to Virgin Trains, crosses Long Marton viaduct at 14.33 heading the 13.52 Carlisle–Preston on Sunday 8 February 2004. This transparency was taken just before its catastrophic failure and subsequent withdrawal from service, so it is quite possibly the last one to be taken of it in service. It languished at Carlisle Upperby depot until November 2005, when it was towed away for scrap at T. J. Thompson at Stockton. It entered traffic at Tinsley TMD in October 1964 as D1779 and was a popular Stratford Brush for over a decade as 47184/47585 *County of Cambridgeshire*, between 1978 and 1988. [6]

Erroneously bearing the 'Scarborough Spa Express' headboard, Royal Scot Class 4-6-0 No. 46115 *Scots Guardsman* has just emerged from Moorcock Tunnel and forges north at Lunds viaduct, heading the 1Z52 07.08 Lancaster–Carlisle 'Fellsman' charter on Wednesday 26 June 2013. [4]

Stanier Black 5, 4-6-0 45231 *The Sherwood Forester*, heads the 1Z53 15.34 'Fellsman' charter from Carlisle to Lancaster, at the head of Dentdale and approaching the northern portal of the 2,629-yard-long Blea Moor Tunnel, on 3 July 2013. [3]

On a midsummer's day more resembling midwinter, Royal Scot Class 4-6-0 No. 46115 *Scots Guardsman* rounds the curve and speeds through Garsdale station in style on 23 June 2012, confidently in charge of the 1Z79 07.58 Scarborough–Carlisle 'Thames Clyde Express', a West Coast Railway Co. private charter with an unusually short trailing load of just seven coaches. [4]

Stanier 8F 2-8-0 No. 48151 plods across Batty Moss viaduct, Ribblehead, working the 1Z22 08.08 Lancaster–Carlisle 'Fellsman' charter on 18 August 2010. [3]

In stunning early evening light, DBS 66162 impressively powers away from Moorcock tunnel and Lunds viaduct in charge of the 4S00 Clitheroe–Mossend loaded with cement on Wednesday 28 August 2013. [4]

Approaching the North Yorkshire/Cumbria county boundary, DBS 66014 heads the 4S62 Milford–Hunterston coal empties at White Birks Common, on the final part of the climb to Ais Gill summit, on Wednesday 28 August 2013. [4]

Watched keenly by a group of walkers on the start of their high-level trek taking in Whernside, Freightliner Heavyhaul 66520 powers north off Batty Moss viaduct, Ribblehead, in charge of the 4S11 Drax–Killoch coal empties on 8 August 2012. [3]

With effect from Monday 29 July, the weekdays-only 6K05 12.18 Carlisle Yard–Crewe Basford Hall Yard Network Rail 'NDS' service contract passed over to Direct Rail Services, in addition to other flows based from the Carlisle Yard 'Virtual Quarry'. During the first week in the hands of DRS, operation 66428 was captured near Risehill Tunnel with a uniform load of ballast gondola wagons on Wednesday 31 July 2013. Rise Hill, also known as Black Moss tunnel, is 1,213 yards in length and the line curves at the north end. It is second only to Blea Moor in terms of length and takes the Settle–Carlisle Line from Dentdale into Garsdale. [4]

It was exactly forty-five years on from that melancholy occasion in August 1968 as BR Standard Class Britannia Pacific No. 70013 *Oliver Cromwell* crossed Dandry Mire viaduct in fine style, heading the northbound Liverpool Lime Street–Carlisle '15 Guinea Special' on Sunday 11 August 2013. [4]

The prospect of two Stanier Black 5s working the 1T57 'Fellsman' in a remote location high on the ridge skirting the head of Dentdale and beneath Widdale Fell, despite the potential lack of exhaust from two locos working up the relatively tame 1 in 264 gradient, was too much of a temptation to resist on Wednesday 7 August 2013. From this eyrie-like position above Dentdale, in real mountain country, the locomotives could be seen bursting out of Blea Moor tunnel and eventually crossing the stunning Arten Gill viaduct. Continuing on their way, they whistled for the boarded crossing at Dent station, the highest station in England at 1,150 feet. This was indeed a sight and an experience to behold. No. 44932, with suitable '1T57' train reporting number board on the smokebox door, pilots 45231 *The Sherwood Forester*, heading the Lancaster–Carlisle '15 Guinea Fellsman', some forty-five years on from the 1968 farewell to BR steam charter. [4]

The conditions we all dream of on the Settle–Carlisle Line: on 12 October 2013, and with precious little sunshine to be experienced, the clouds parted at just the right moment. With Garsdale opening up beyond, Stanier Coronation Pacific No. 46233 *Duchess of Sutherland* approaches the site of the former water troughs, heading the Down 'Thames Clyde Express', in effect the 1Z55 05.20 Lincoln–Carlisle charter, on 12 October 2013. [4]

Struggling to maintain its grip on the greasy rails, Stanier Coronation Pacific No. 46233 *Duchess of Sutherland* storms past Angerholme on the final assault on the summit at Ais Gill, heading the return 'Thames Clyde Express' charter, the 1Z34 14.40 Carlisle–Lincoln, on Saturday 12 October 2013. [5]

Virgin Class 47/8 47841 *Spirit of Chester* heads a northbound Virgin Trains morning service, diverted via the Settle–Carlisle route, through the mist at Bullgill on 16 February 2002. Beyond the arch, the road has been traditionally guarded by two unfriendly looking dogs, with the length of their tethers carefully gauged to allow walkers a fine line to pass through the centre of them on the road without a mishap occurring. [5]

In atrociously wet conditions, Freightliner Heavyhaul's 66615 is heading a very late 6M11 Hunterston–Fiddler's Ferry loaded with coal, seen breasting the summit near Ais Gill Cottages and the county boundary between Cumbria and Yorkshire on Thursday 15 August 2013. [4]

On Wednesday 10 July 2013, DBS 66100 crosses Dandry Mire (Moorcock) viaduct heading the 6M00 Mossend–Clitheroe empty cement tankers, viewed through an arch beneath the former Hawes branch line, just before the former Hawes Junction, after which the station at Garsdale was originally named. [4]

The southernmost of the three Blea Moor Tunnel ventilation shafts, visibly doing what it was designed to do almost 140 years on, with diesel fumes clearly emanating from the shaft following the passage of a Carlisle–Leeds diesel passenger service on Wednesday 24 July 2013. The tunnel was built with the aid of the three 10-foot-diameter shafts, and the granite extracted during the construction work can be seen in this view – the heaps on the hillside below the middle of the three shafts. This nearest one is 217 feet deep. Hundreds of navvies dug the tunnel out by hand, using steam engines at the top of the seven shafts along the length of the tunnel to haul out the spoil. Terrible weather took its toll, with several men drowned in the cuttings on Blea Moor during a rainstorm in July 1870, and snow and floods holding up the work over the following two years. The first passage through was completed by August 1873, and the arching and lining was completed by November 1874. The trackbed of the 1,900-metre-long tramway that transported spoil up to six huge spoil heaps is still visible, as are two oblong quarries with an associated trackway that terminates close to the tramway. Brick to line the tunnel was produced at the brickworks sited near to the Ribblehead viaduct, and three shafts were left to ventilate the tunnel. [3]

The Force Gill aqueduct was built by the Midland Railway in 1870 to carry the waters from Force Gill into Dale Beck across the line below the southern entrance to Blea Moor Tunnel, situated below to the left in this viewpoint and looking towards Pen-y-ghent on the horizon. The aqueduct had been refurbished during Railtrack's custodianship, and originally a concrete channel was planned, but after an appropriate uproar this sympathetic reconstruction was undertaken. The unprecedented scarcity of rainfall over the preceding weeks in summer 2013 had left the water level of Force Gill through the channel less rapid than is normally seen. [3]

The return leg of the 1T57 '15 Guinea Fellsman' charter from Carlisle to Lancaster on Wednesday 7 August 2013 emerges from the dank environs of the 2,629-yard-long Blea Moor, with Stanier Black 5s 44932 and 45231 in charge. They are passing beneath the Force Gill aqueduct seen on the opposite page. Some two hours after this train had passed through the tunnel, the service train in which the author returned to Carlisle took in some of the remaining smoke in the tunnel through the open top light windows, and an impressive amount of smoke was also forced out of the northern portal as the train emerged, evoking childhood steam-age memories. [3]

Royal Scot Class 4-6-0 46115 *Scots Guardsman* bursts out of the northern portal of Blea Moor tunnel into Dentdale, heading the 1Z80 08.58 York–Carlisle 'Waverley' charter on 15 August 2010. [3]

Stanier Jubilee 45699 *Galatea* emerges from Blea Moor tunnel's southern portal, heading the return 1Z53 15.34 Carlisle–Lancaster 'Fellsman' charter on Wednesday 17 July 2013. [3]

Stanier Black 5, 4-6-0 No. 45231 *The Sherwood Forester*, emerges from Moorcock Tunnel, crossing Lunds viaduct, heading the 1Z52 07.08 Lancaster–Carlisle 'Fellsman' charter on Wednesday 31 July 2013. [4]

With Ingleborough standing sentinel in the low clouds behind, and intermittent sunshine illuminating Chapel-le-Dale in the valley below, Gresley K4 Class 2-6-0 No. 61994 *The Great Marquess* gets stuck into the 1 in 100 climb away from the 30 mph speed restriction at Batty Moss viaduct, Ribblehead, and passes Blea Moor signal box heading the 1Z52 07.08 Lancaster–Carlisle 'Fellsman' charter on 8 August 2012. [3]

Brush Type 4/Class 47, No. 47580 *County of Essex*, is piloted by Gresley K4 2-6-0 No. 61994 *The Great Marquess* between Blea Moor and Ribblehead while heading the return 1Z53 15.34 Carlisle–Lancaster 'Fellsman' on Wednesday 24 July 2013. [3]

A fleeting glimpse of EWS 37408 *Loch Rannoch* heading a Leeds–Carlisle Arriva Trains service at speed past Long Strumble farm near Cotehill in the heavy rain on 20 December 2003. [9]

On 22 December 2003, Freightliner Heavyhaul 66556 runs down the grade from Ais Gill at Low Frith with coal empties for Carlisle Yard. [5]

Res-liveried 47784 and Inter-City-liveried 47826 head over Armathwaite viaduct with the 1S55 11.28 Virgin Trains Preston–Carlisle, diverted via the Settle–Carlisle line, on 4 January 2010. The viaduct, now mainly concealed by trees, is 80 feet high, has nine arches and was built between 1871 and 1874. [8]

In a brief shaft of sunlight which followed a heavy shower, EWS 47792 *Robin Hood* was captured at Durranhill powering away from the Border City and Petteril Bridge Junction, heading the diverted 1V66 13.52 Carlisle–Preston on 11 January 2004, the eventual departure time being almost one hour late. The former steam motive power depot was located to the left of this view, and the once-extensive Midland Railway goods yard and shed are to the centre right. [9]

In an unexpected spell of sunlight, Stanier Black 5, 45157 *The Lancashire Fusilier* (aka 45407), heads across Batty Moss viaduct with the 09.10 Liverpool Lime Street–Carlisle 'Cumbrian Fellsman' charter on 21 October 2000. Batty Moss (otherwise known as Ribblehead viaduct) is the Settle–Carlisle Line's best-known structure, its twenty-four lofty arches spanning the shakehole pockmarks of Batty Moss bog. [3]

Upon the successful completion of much of the track refurbishment work, which culminated in a four-week possession of the Settle–Carlisle line in November 2000, Railtrack decided to mark the event and generate some positive publicity by agreeing to operate a steam-hauled ballast train from Hellifield to Carlisle using David Smith's 8F Class 2-8-0 freight locomotive No. 48151. The purpose was to remove stockpiled ballast remaining from the PW engineering work. On 19 December 2000, having had its empty wagons loaded at the siding, the 8F slowly gets under way from Ribblehead siding with the heavy load, the 7P50 12.57 Ribblehead–Carlisle yard, comprising twenty 'Dogfish' stone hopper wagons and two brakevans. [3]

Stanier Jubilee Class 4-6-0 45699 *Galatea* heads the 1Z42 16.22 Carlisle–Broxbourne 'Cathedrals Express' high above the Eden Valley, between Dry Beck and Armathwaite on Wednesday 5 March 2014. [8]

Bulleid Merchant Navy Class Pacific 35005 *Canadian Pacific* at bridge 137, otherwise known as Ais Gill viaduct, heading a return 'Cumbrian Mountain Express' charter from Carlisle to London Euston on 29 May 1999. [5]

In pouring rain and with clouds hanging low over Thwaite Bridge Common, Royal Scot Class 4-6-0 No. 46115 *Scots Guardsman* approaches the North Yorkshire/Cumbria border at Shaw Paddock, just before Ais Gill summit, heading the 1Z70 09.13 York–Carlisle 'Waverley' charter on Sunday 5 August 2012. The Scot regrettably was declared a failure at Carlisle and the passengers experienced West Coast Railway Company Class 47 haulage for their return journey to Yorkshire. [4]

Stanier Coronation Class 4-6-2 No. 46233 *Duchess of Sutherland* puts everything she has into the final few hundred yards of climb approaching the summit of Ais Gill on Wednesday 22 May 2012. The accomplished fireman-ship at just the right moment produced a satisfying amount of exhaust for this early summer 12°C temperature. This particular location on the Settle–Carlisle Line was a firm favourite with the renowned photographer Rt Revd Eric Treacy. [4]

On Wednesday 1 August 2012, Gresley K4 2-6-0 No. 61994 *The Great Marquess* is seen crossing Ais Gill viaduct in the driving rain heading the 1Z53 15.34 Carlisle–Lancaster 'Fellsman' charter on the final section of the 1 in 100 climb to Ais Gill summit, its first run over the Settle–Carlisle in recent years in preservation. She was built at Darlington and introduced to service in June 1938 for passenger traffic on the West Highland Line. During the 1950s, the K4's sphere of operation enlarged and they began to appear at locations such as Edinburgh, Perth, Forfar, Ayr and Tweedmouth. In 1959 they were all concentrated at Thornton Junction depot in Fife and all were withdrawn by the end of 1961, 61994 being the final class member surviving in BR service. [5]

To the delight of all present, a shaft of sunlight just catches the 1Z73 15.45 Carlisle–York 'Waverley' approaching Ais Gill summit, with Stanier Black 5 No. 44932 in charge, on 2 September 2012. [4]

Rarely are evenings at Blea Moor as idyllic as this. The perfect summer's evening showcases the mass of Ingleborough looming over Chapel-le-Dale and Batty Moss viaduct. DBS 66103 labours up the 1 in 100 grade past Blea Moor signal box, heading the 4S00 loaded cement tankers from Clitheroe–Mossend on 17 July 2013. [3]

Baugh Fell looms above DBS 66103 heading the 4M00 Mossend–Clitheroe empty cement, passing the former Midland Railway cottages at Garsdale on Wednesday 24 July 2013. [4]

DBS 66197 passes the remains of the snowdrift screens high above Dentdale at High Thistletwaite, heading a long and well-loaded 6K05 12.18 Carlisle–Crewe Basford Hall engineer's service on Wednesday 17 July 2013, shortly before the contract for this NDS service was handed over to DRS. [4]

The giant hogweed in the boggy ground at Ais Gill summit sets the scene for DBS 66102 approaching the summit, heading the 6K05 12.18 Carlisle Yard–Crewe Basford Hall engineer's service on 1 September 2010. [4]

The north-easterly wind whipping the exhaust right over the train on the sunny side was not to be an issue on a very dull 10 July 2013. Stanier 8F 2-8-0 No. 48151 scurries across Dandry Mire viaduct with the 'Fellsman' charter, the 1Z72 07.08 from Lancaster to Carlisle. [4]

Conditions do not come much better than this in the upper Eden and it was a joy to be out to witness Royal Scot Class 4-6-0 No. 46115 *Scots Guardsman* doing what she is best at: tackling the 1 in 100 climb. With a further 5 miles to go at predominantly the same gradient before reaching Ais Gill summit, the Scot is seen at Bullgill heading in fine style the 1Z87 return 'Winter Cumbrian Mountain Express' charter, the 14.44 Carlisle–London Euston on Saturday 1 March 2014. [5]

Stanier Royal Scot Class 4-6-0 No. 46115 *Scots Guardsman* crosses Ais Gill viaduct while heading the return 1Z87 14.28 Carlisle–London Euston 'Cumbrian Mountain Express' on Thursday 20 June 2013. [5]

The driver of Royal Scot Class 4-6-0 No. 46115 *Scots Guardsman* was extracting everything the loco had to give as the 1Z89 14.27 Carlisle–London Euston 'Cumbrian Mountain Express' approached Armathwaite Tunnel in the pouring rain on Wednesday 16 October 2013. The noise of the exhaust was deafening and even the fireman was to be seen shielding his ears as the loco plunged into the darkness of the first of three tunnels within 1 mile through the Baron Wood Estate. [8]

With the splendour of Dentdale opening up beyond, DBS 66100 heads the 4M00 07.05 Mossend–Clitheroe empty cement tankers at Harber Gill on Wednesday 7 August 2013. [4]

DRS 66432 trundles through the delightful former Westmorland county town station of Appleby while heading the 6K05 12.18 Carlisle Yard–Crewe Basford Hall engineer's service on 14 August 2013. It is easy to see in this view the scale of the platforms, built for Anglo-Scottish express trains, and that the station buildings are constructed from brick rather than stone. The circular plaque on the side of the Up station building commemorates 'The Rt Revd Eric Treacy MBE LLD, Lord Bishop of Wakefield 1968–1976, railway photographer, pastor to railwaymen and lover of life and railways, who sadly died on Appleby station on 13 May 1978'. Appleby is one of the major stations on the route, with long platforms ideal for charter trains, a metal footbridge, and a water tank and crane to service the steam charter trains. [6]

Sun at the right time calls for much luck around Blea Moor and Dentdale, and no sooner had DRS 66431, heading the 6K05 12.18 Carlisle Yard–Crewe on 7 August 2013, passed into the northern portal of Blea Moor tunnel than shadows covered the foreground scene. The rear of the train has just cleared Dent Head viaduct, spanning the infant River Dee. Comprising ten arches, it is some 1,150 feet above sea level. [3]

Low cloud hangs over Wild Boar Fell, however a fleeting shaft of sunlight spotlights Colas Rail's Class 56 Grid No. 56105 making a grand entrance at Shaw Paddock, now running down the grade, heading the 6J37 Carlisle Yard–Chirk log train on Thursday 15 August 2013. [4]

Gresley K4 Class 2-6-0 No. 61994 *The Great Marquess* climbs through the Mallerstang valley towards the summit of Ais Gill heading the 1Z53 15.34 Carlisle–Lancaster 'Fellsman' charter on 8 August 2012. [5]

The dark clouds hanging over Angram Common and the limestone ridge of Hangingstone Scar set the scene for Gresley K4 No. 61994 *The Great Marquess* heading the return 'Fellsman', the 1Z53 15.34 Carlisle–Lancaster charter over Ais Gill viaduct, on 8 August 2012. [5]

Royal Scot Class 4-6-0 No. 46115 *Scots Guardsman* leans to the curve on the 1 in 132 climb south through Armathwaite station heading the return 1Z71 'Waverley' charter to York, the 15.45 from Carlisle, on Sunday 28 July 2013. The 'Waverley', originally called the 'Thames-Forth Express', was an express passenger train operating over the Midland Main Line from London St Pancras to Edinburgh Waverley. The original name was given to the morning departure from London by the London, Midland & Scottish Railway in September 1927. Its sister train to Glasgow, which departed an hour later, was named the 'Thames–Clyde Express'. The 'Waverley' travelled by the scenic Settle–Carlisle route, but could not compete on speed to Scotland with the trains travelling on the East Coast Main Line via York. As a result, after the 1920s few passengers travelled the full length of the route. The 'Thames-Forth Express' lost its title at the outbreak of the Second World War, in common with almost all named trains in the UK, and a name was not restored until June 1957, when it was renamed 'The Waverley'. It provided a useful service from the East Midlands and Yorkshire to Edinburgh, and also provided a direct London service to the small towns on the Settle–Carlisle route, and in the Scottish borders between Carlisle and Edinburgh (the Waverley Route). However, by this time the train had acquired a bad reputation for slowness and unpunctuality. It ceased to run during the winter after 1964, but continued to operate during the summer months until September 1968. The revival of 'The Waverley' in recent years, operating only during the summer holiday, is therefore wholly appropriate and a delight to see. [8]

With safety valves feathering, the fireman of the 1Z53 15.34 Carlisle–Lancaster 'Fellsman' charter on Wednesday 26 June 2013 has decided to take a well-earned rest from shovelling coal. Royal Scot Class 4-6-0 No. 46115 *Scots Guardsman* is passing Angerholme and has almost reached Ais Gill summit. [5]

A Carlisle–Leeds Northern Rail service climbs the last mile towards Ais Gill summit near Angerholme on 3 December 2012. [5]

Due to shortage of rolling stock, London Midland City single unit No. 153366 was acquired on temporary loan by Northern Rail, and is at Horton-in-Ribblesdale station on 19 June 2011, at the rear augmenting a Class 158 forming a Leeds–Carlisle service. Horton station, closed in 1970 and reopened in 1986, offers a superb view of Pen-y-ghent and is a favourite disembarkation point for walkers undertaking the 'Three Peaks' walk, a total of 24 miles. The station, which at one time won the area's best-kept station award for seventeen consecutive years, was fully renovated by the Friends of the Settle–Carlisle. [2]

EWS 66064 crosses Dent Head viaduct working the Drax–Newbiggin carrying containerised gypsum on 26 June 1999. The viaduct, at 100 feet high and 199 yards in length, spans the infant River Dee and is built at some 1,150 feet above sea level. [3]

Almost centipede-like, Freightliner Heavyhaul's 66526 labours away from Dent station near the curiously named Rotten Bottom, the name given to the location of the abandoned farmhouse on the slopes of Widdale Fell. The 6M11 Hunterston–Fiddlers Ferry loaded coal hoppers on Wednesday 7 August 2013. [4]

Peppercorn K1 2-6-0 No. 62012 (aka 62005) rounds the curve from Blackburn and into Hellifield station heading the 'Lancashire Witch', the 1Z72, the second circular charter of the day from Carnforth on 16 October 2004. Situated 231 miles from London St Pancras via the Midland route, this junction station used to be of great importance with a locomotive shed and extensive goods facilities, with exchange traffic between the Midland and Lancashire & Yorkshire railways, employing almost three-quarters of the town's population. The station has been painstakingly restored and the tea room there maintains a tradition of a bygone age on the railway. [1]

Stanier Black 5, 4-6-0 No. 44932, climbing the 1 in 100 grade past Watershed Mill, near Settle, heading the 1Z70 09.13 York–Carlisle 'Waverley' on Sunday 2 September 2012. There are three paper mills in this vicinity, but Watershed Mill has been redeveloped to house a number of speciality shops and factory outlets. [2]

Braving the driving rain, the driver of LMS Jubilee Class 4-6-0 No. 5690 *Leander*, Driver Gordon Hodgson, leans out of his cab window and watches for the 'right away' signal from Carlisle Citadel station for the 1Z25 15.19 Carlisle–Lancaster 'Fellsman' charter service on 28 July 2010. [9]

Stanier Black 5, 4-6-0 No. 45231 *The Sherwood Forester*, works down the 1 in 264 grade skirting the eastern edge of Dentdale above Harbourgill with the 1Z53 15.34 Carlisle–Lancaster 'Fellsman' charter on Wednesday 3 July 2013. [4]

Stanier 8P Pacific 46233 *Duchess of Sutherland* stretches her legs and puts out a fine exhaust on the level, heading the 1Z55 14.25 Carlisle–Preston leg of the 'Great Britain V' railtour past the Howe & Co. sidings on 26 April 2012. [9]

BR 8P Pacific No. 71000 *Duke of Gloucester* emerges from the rain into a brief spell of sunshine at Greengate, south of Kirkby Stephen, heading the 1Z72 14.31 Carlisle–Gloucester 'Cumbrian Mountain Express' on 21 May 2011. [5]

Royal Scot Class 4-6-0 No. 46115 *Scots Guardsman* climbing up to Low House crossing from Dry Beck viaduct, heading a Spitfire Tours 1Z31 05.21 Worcester Shrub Hill–Carlisle 'Settle & Carlisle Flyer' on a rather overcast 1 June 2011. [8]

Gresley K4 2-6-0 No. 61994 *The Great Marquess* on the climb to Ais Gill summit at Shoregill, high above Pendragon Castle and Outhgill, heading the return 1Z53 15.34 Carlisle–Lancaster 'Fellsman' charter on Wednesday 14 August 2013. [5]

Colas Rail's 56087 and 56105 approach Dandry Mire viaduct, Garsdale, heading the 6J37 Carlisle Yard–Chirk timber on Wednesday 10 July 2013. [4]

The driver of DRS 66434 (still bearing the Jarvis Fastline decals and on spot-hire to Colas Rail) climbs into the cab at Ribblehead Sidings in order to 'prep' his engine prior to departing, via a run-round at Blea Moor, for Chirk with the 6Z37 loaded with timber on 21 May 2011. [3]

Colas Rail's Class 66/8 No. 66842 approaches Ais Gill summit heading the 6J37 Carlisle Yard–Chirk (Kronospan) loaded with timber on 10 November 2010. [4]

The sound of the approaching timber train is deafening when combined with the noise of the gushing water of Ais Gill Beck, flowing on beneath Ais Gill viaduct and feeding into the fledgling River Eden deep in the valley beyond. The rain is sheeting across Mallerstang Edge as Colas Rail's 66848 labours up the final mile, the relentless 1 in 100 climb to Ais Gill summit, heading the 6J37 Carlisle Yard–Chirk (Kronospan) timber train on 4 July 2012. [5]

Stanier Jubilee Class 4-6-0 No. 45699 *Galatea* caught in the low autumn sunlight at Duncowfold, heading the return 'Cumbrian Jubilee' charter, the 1Z46 14.40 Carlisle–Tyseley Warwick Road on Saturday 9 November 2013. [9]

The gorse is vibrant and at its best, but there is still very little sign of foliage on the broadleaf trees with the summer solstice closely approaching. Coronation Pacific No. 46233 *Duchess of Sutherland* makes easy work of the 1 in 330 climb to Wastebank Tunnel heading the 1Z89 14.28 Carlisle–London Euston 'Cumbrian Mountain Express' charter on Wednesday 22 May 2013. [7]

Stanier Black 5, 4-6-0 No. 45305, crossing Crosby Garrett viaduct heading the return Carlisle–Liverpool Lime Street 'Cumbrian Mountain Express' charter on a very wet Saturday 6 August 2011. The viaduct is 55 feet high and 110 yards long, the stone for its construction having been hewn from the adjacent cutting. [5]

Stanier Royal Scot Class 4-6-0 No. 46115 *Scots Guardsman* crossed Crosby Garrett viaduct with the 1Z87 14.44 Carlisle–Farington Junction and London Euston 'Cumbrian Mountain Express' just before the sun dipped behind the hill on Saturday 15 February 2014. [5]

The wind and the rain are lashing across Batty Moss as Stanier Class 8F 2-8-0 No. 48151 gets to grips with its heavy stone train, the 7P50 Ribblehead sidings–Carlisle Yard ballast train, crossing Batty Moss viaduct on Tuesday 19 December 2000. The wind velocity was so strong that the exhaust was easily carried in front of the locomotive. A steam-hauled ballast train heading over the Settle–Carlisle Line in the twenty-first century was very much a not-to-be-missed, once-in-a-lifetime opportunity. Railtrack chartered LMS Stanier-designed Heavy Freight 8F 2-8-0 No. 48151 from the West Coast Railway Company at Carnforth, which took a train of twenty empty hoppers from Hellifield to Ribblehead for loading, then forwarded them to Carlisle in appalling weather. This event was to mark the reopening of the Settle–Carlisle Line after its major refurbishment. [3]

In a scene befitting a Harry Potter film, Hall Class 4-6-0 No. 5972 *Olton Hall,* star locomotive of the films, heads the 12.06 Hellifield–Carlisle 'Christmas Special' charter across Batty Moss viaduct, Ribblehead, on 18 December 1999. [3]